how to survive yourself

marina aimée

how to survive yourself copyright © 2022 by
Marina Aimée. Second Edition, revised in 2023.
No part of this book may be used or reproduced in any
manner whatsoever without written permission.

@marinaaimeepoetry

Poems, cover and illustrations by Marina Aimée

ISBN: 9798830122122

Marina Aimée was born in the Spanish Mediterranean in 1997. She self-published a poetry book in Spanish in 2020, *Ojalá te atragantes de mí*. By the time this book is published she lives in San Francisco but her plan is to travel and live in as many places as she can. She grew up surrounded by love, kindness and freedom and over the years has learned how to love and comprehend herself. She's still living a beautiful and hard journey of healing and self-love, but at least she survived herself.

you can find her poetry in English on Instagram and TikTok: @marinaaimeepoetry

table of contents

slash 9
buried 35
sprinkle 69
blossom 109

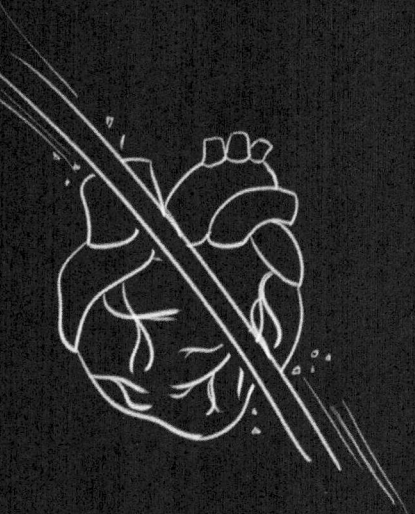

slash

i've spent years trying to find a place to feel at peace
but how to find it if i'm always at war with myself?

how can you ask another person to complete you
if you're the one with the power to heal yourself?

how can you demand a city to change you
if you're the only one that doesn't want to evolve?

how can you expect things to be different
if you're always quiet and static and scared?

how can you look for peace outside during the day
if every night you start the war inside?

how to survive yourself

lots of memories on the floor
just looking at me
as if i could do something
to bury them under the pain

blue and purple fire through the air
just trying to burn me
as if i had enough time
to start again without failing

hundreds of lies around the corner
just waiting for me
as if i could arrive safe and whole
to the next line of this poem

a huge amount of fear in my hands
just screaming at me
as if i could be prepared anytime
to close my eyes and make it disappear

my mind is detached from
every part of my body
so i cannot feel any pain
when i'm tearing apart
the pieces of myself
that i hate the most
i live inside an
uninhabited shell
cutting the pieces
i cannot recognize
scared that i'm gonna
bleed to death with
the next bite that goes
straight for the jugular

i try to stop this anxiety
that's squeezing my throat
as if it wanted to strangle me
so i don't breathe this toxic air
full of lies that the society
is blowing in my stunned face

i make an effort to stop
these iron and heavy feet
that want to step on me
crush me into the floor
forbid me to inhale again

i make an effort
to hold hands with reality
i want it to look me in the eye
so i can beg to slow down
the frenetic rhythm of my life
i don't want to run anymore
i don't want to collide with what's
waiting at the end of the fall

i pray to all the gods i don't believe in
so they can help me to understand
what's happening in this foul society
full of lies and fake friends
but anxiety doesn't stop
and it keeps choking me

instead of stopping
those iron and heavy feet
climb on my back

marina aimée

and step harder and harder

instead of holding hands
and looking at me
and listening to my plea
reality goes faster and harder

instead of answering my prayers
those gods i don't believe in
aren't listening to me
so i don't understand anything

here i am
splashed into the floor
without knowing how to stop
lost and alone and fractured

is this the day i'll finally
be brave enough?

i try to span more than my soul can hold
i keep going silently instead of shouting
i look in the mirror with clenched teeth
i hold the world on my scratched hands

when am i going to stop trying to kill myself with all
this pressure?

i've always tried to enjoy to the bone
every ephemeral moment of happiness
and when the enjoyment transforms into
knives in the stomach and choked throats
and tears of blood menace to overflow me
i transform my agony into broken poetry

i've always been good at writing
from pain and sadness and rage
i got used to feel it and transform it
and today i'm not able to create
when i feel happy and blessed
i just know how to heal my soreness
with words and spit out everything
i cannot express in any other way

–pain is transitory and unavoidable

nothing can return me the freedom
i lost when you put your dirty hands
on my blameless intimacy
it doesn't matter how hard i try
to liberate myself
to forgive myself
i keep blaming myself
even if i was unarmed
i keep seeing you
when i close my eyes
i keep hating you
despite i know it's not the way
i keep trying
so so hard to forget your touch
and without a hint of doubt
i swear to you:

one day
you'll disappear from me

how to survive yourself

the more i fight to be who they want me to be
the more i get away from who i really am

morning coffee grounds
spilled on the kitchen table
your old black t-shirt
covering my cold body
our favorite song playing
out loud all over the house
your voice rumbling in my ears
repeating *you're not enough*
my trembling arms holding
the smashed pieces of my reality
the silent bang of your goodbye
tattooed with fire in my pupils
my legs crashing into the floor
begging you to come back
and your last words destroying
everything i've been fighting for

i don't love you anymore
and i'm not sorry for that

i would like to tell him
that i'm not scared because of something he did
i'm freaking out
because of everything others did to me before

i've always smelled goodbyes from afar
i've always known when a farewell was near
i've always been able to anticipate pain
so i shrink into myself and cry measureless
then i become authentic diamond armor
indestructible and icy and imperishable
that's how the ending usually hits me
without changing anything in my core
without moving me an inch from here
this defensive position i've created
that's how i learned to live a farewell:
crying entire oceans before it arrives

anxiety is like that
you cannot always control it
some days you need to rest
breathe until you calm down
in the days you feel alone
broken
perturbed
miserable
you really need to believe
the most important thing
in the entire world
is your next breath
and then you realize
you can actually do it
inhaling in 4
holding in 7
exhaling in 8
some days
you need to stop
thinking
believing
fighting

–just stop and keep breathing

i've spent thousands of nights
going to sleep unsatisfied
my heart is a mess and my mind
isn't always working properly
i just think about running away
going back home as soon as possible
i'm scared he was the love of my life
even if i don't believe in *romantic love*
i cry in silence any time i need to
and i talk too loud for this quiet city

—intrusive thoughts

how to survive yourself

don't fall in love
with your idea of someone
your expectations aren't
the reality about that person

i used to think that love
was the most powerful feeling
it's so strong it can transform you
into a better version of yourself
it's also influential enough
to destroy you into ashes
but i've been telling myself
maybe the most potent feeling
is actually hope since it's
resilient and massive enough
to make you wait forever
but also capable of killing you
when what you deserve never arrives
and you remain still and quiet
just waiting and hoping forever

–hope can keep you alive
but also destroy you

how to survive yourself

when you end a relationship
you don't just lose the other person
you lose plans and expectations
you lose a part of who you are
because that version of yourself
that existed with the other person
cannot exist again in the same way
that's why you're so sad and broken
because you lost your couple
but a part of who you were is gone too

you're not just missing that person
you're missing yourself too

i know exactly what i need to do
but i'm so afraid of failure
that i cannot even try

how to survive yourself

wake up in the morning and make that effort to get out from under the sheets. i know you want to stay in that safe place. i know. trust me. but you can do it. i know you can. take a cold or hot shower. pick what you really want and deserve. don't pick one choice or another because you want to punish yourself. just take care of your body and your mind. remember: *mente sana in corpore sano*. let the water wash away all your bad thoughts. treat yourself with an abundant breakfast. choose your favorite fruit. add some chocolate if you need to. prepare a coffee as you like it best. eat with no hurry and relish. you deserve to enjoy your meal without anxiety. without counting calories. without guilt. just pleasure. read a book. paint something. write. listen to music. dance. whatever fits you better. but connect with your creative part, with your feelings and emotions, and express them. let them go. work out. run. go for a walk. practice yoga. meditate. move your body. connect with it. go somewhere you like to be. a garden. a beach. a park. a mountain. indulge yourself with nature. let the sun bless you with new energies. go to your favorite restaurant and ask for that special drink and food. talk with friends. laugh with family. visit your therapist. call someone if you don't want to be alone. whenever you think of hurting yourself, take a deep breath. then another one. breathe again. you can do it. you can survive this. remember: your body is your home. self-care is the solution. self-love is the right path. hurting yourself is not going to improve anything. you deserve to be happy and loved and safe and fulfilled. you deserve to take care of yourself. you deserve to love yourself everyday. even in your worst day. especially then. i know you're scared. i know you're mainly scared of everything you know you can do. but you need to trust in yourself. darkness won't last forever. you'll see the light again. you'll be happy again. you need to keep going. you need to survive yourself. keep walking. keep living. you have infinite reasons to do it.

—one day taking care of yourself

how to survive yourself

i tiptoe around the memories
trying not to make noise
so i don't wake up all the monsters
who have become dust under my bed

marina aimée

you'll always come back
to the places that destroyed you

buried

today i read a quote that unsettled me
have you healed or are you just
trying to not think about it?
i swear to you it has pierced me
as if it was an irrefutable doubt
how could i know if i'm unbroken if
i don't think i've ever been whole before?
which is the clue that will make me see
that i have healed
that i have forgotten
maybe i'll never figure out what truly means to heal
maybe i'll never understand if i'm unscratched
the difference between before and now
is that today i'm able to love myself like this
even if i'm shattered

how to survive yourself

we spend an incredible amount of time
overthinking and worrying about everything

past and future and aspirations
friends and parents and relationships
college and money and work
travels and media and public image

we spend our life imagining scenarios
that aren't real anywhere but in our minds
crying for people who don't deserve our love
fighting for a dream we can't even remember

we waste our time worrying instead of living
we miss our lives because we're too busy
trying to figure out how to be enough
and we don't even know for whom

my question here is:
is it worth it?
not for me anymore

he was the first, only and last time
i called someone *love*

it was an October night at 2am
he came closer to my ear
and started reciting a poem
the same i have stuck in my chest
since he made me feel goosebumps

–Aniversario

maybe the persistent fight
to find true happiness
is exactly what takes us away
from the real blessedness

maybe the constant effort
to reach an invisible goal
puts us on the opposite side
of where true blissfulness is

—don't battle so hard to find happiness
just learn how to feel it

how to survive yourself

it's been a while since
you disappeared from my life
but i still find you
in every new person i meet

how am i supposed to
tolerate other's hands
if i still have yours
on every part of my body

how am i supposed to
love other's kisses
if i still feel your tongue
in all my broken nights

how am i supposed to
touch another soul
if i still remember exactly
how to understand yours

it's been months since
you let our story go
but i still feel you
in every new person i try to love

and you cannot imagine how painful it is
and you cannot imagine how unfair it is

when you left i got a new tattoo
that will always remind me of you
just in case you decide to come back
because i need something stronger
than my hurt mind to remember
all the pain you made me go through

are you so worried trying to
understand life that you're missing it?

you'll want to leave
when i open the closet
to say goodnight
to all my monsters

you'll leave
in silence or making noise
when you understand
that i live attached to the chains
of what one day i did to myself

how to survive yourself

can you remember
how beautiful it was?
here and now
sitting on our beach
i'm wondering
if you still think about me
if you feel your heart beating
when you hear my name

i keep asking myself
if you try to find me on other lips
if you also close your eyes at night
to feel our story again and again

i would like to know
if you still find me in every sunrise
because i still find you in every sunset

only when they ripped me apart from the outside
was i able to heal myself from the inside

in Spain we have a proverb
mejor tarde que nunca
'it's better being late than never arriving'
but let me tell you something that life taught me:

sometimes, being late is like never arriving at all

decisions are everywhere
challenging me
changing my life
presenting millions
of possibilities daily

decisions are all around me
some of them extremely easy
and others too difficult to confront

at the end of the day what matters
is what you have already decided
not all the possible scenarios
that you're not going to live

—so stop worrying

parts of my mind and body and soul feel
i miss you every day of every week
i miss what we were and what we had
i miss all our silent poems and loud songs
i miss holding hands and kissing your eyes
i miss your limitless way of loving me

but how can i dare to tell you about these feelings
if i'm not even sure if at some point i loved you
in the same immeasurable way that you did
if i'm not even sure if i'm really missing you
or i just miss your pure and noble sincere love

when you leave just make sure
you're not running away

−especially from yourself

how to survive yourself

i don't want to lose myself again
to disappear in the middle of all
the awesome things i'm living

i don't want to lose what cost me
an unimaginable effort
to find
to build
to see
to love

i'm so sorry
but i cannot lose myself again

if that means i have to lose you
and choose myself
i'll cry your absence
but i'll still be complete

how can i focus on just one thing in this world full of incitements? how can i put the center of attention on one emotion, one dream, one person, when i live surrounded by possibilities? i don't want to choose. i want to accept everything. i want to feel and live it all. who says that i need to pick? why can't i have it all? who forbids me? and the most important question:

what is *all* for me?

how to survive yourself

i learned by force how to take care of myself
i had to discover how to comprehend my mind
i became a master in the art of loving myself
in the most deep and beautiful way

i'm always my best friend no matter what
i give myself the hand instead of the knife
i support my body during bad slumps

but sometimes i lose perspective
i forget how difficult it was to get here
i turn it over and i'm my worst enemy
a fake smile and a blade behind my back

the horrible part of being
my best friend and my worst enemy
is that i'm an expert in being both

at the end of the day it's true
no one can know better than me
all my amazing strengths but also
the thousand weaknesses i try to hide

marina aimée

i've seen the flames of hell in your eyes
how am i supposed to love
any kind of heaven after that?

she was telling me all these stories about her childhood and i was impressed because i don't think i can remember anything about my childhood that clear. i have pieces, little flashes, memories, but not whole stories full of complications. i was looking at her eyes, not tired but full of energy, and i thought *maybe when you get old you start remembering everything that you cannot truly visualize during previous years.* maybe it's a superpower that only grandmas and grandpas have: remembering so they can tell.

what will happen with me since i don't want kids? who am i going to tell my stories to?

it's gonna hurt like hell to see
how you continue your life without me
how you don't need my arms anymore
how you keep walking but not by my side
i'll soon exchange sadness for relief
because today i finally understood
why we need to say goodbye:

i'm not enough for you anymore
and you're too small compared to all my dreams

stop fighting with people who
don't try to get your point
save your energy and words
use them to hear yourself
to heal your body and soul
not to convince someone
that will never use empathy
to be closer to who you are

–run away from people who drain your energy

marina aimée

maybe that's why i write
to tell all my stories
so they don't drown me

how to survive yourself

i work like this
when a love ends
it's absolutely over for me

i don't regret anymore
i cry no more tears
i have no more feelings

i just assumed time ago
that everything has an ending
and it's perfectly normal

am i a bad person
for not having feelings anymore
for someone who's still in love with me?

i feel selfish and ungrateful
but i cannot force my body
heart and mind to feel again

trust me
i tried it before
it doesn't work properly

here i am several months later
remembering what never happened
and living with my whole heart
in the memory of one perfect night
the exact time that this song lasts
when you gonna realize it was just
that the time was wrong, Juliet?
your clear ocean-colored eyes
the city lights flashing under us
your voice singing near my ear
the image of a perfect stranger
who was the love of my life
for just a single healing night

–6:01 minutes

when he comes back
–he will do it–
close your eyes to see
how he treated you
how he made you feel
you're no longer trapped
so do yourself a favor
and quickly run away
in the opposite direction

back in San Francisco after a trip
i decided to text my parents
who were 10000 kilometers away
i'm already safe at home
and a second later i realized: home

how hard it has to be for them
to read that i'm at home
and it's not in their house
and it's not by their side
but how beautiful for me
to say i have a home here

i wonder how many homes
i have all over the world
because being at home is not
entering the door of a house
it's the people you share your life with
it's about a deep feeling in your chest
it's a place with the incredible ability
of waking up all those emotions
that help me to feel alive again

i'm at home
but at the same time
i'll never again have just one home

how to survive yourself

your eyes are telling me more lies
than the ones you can pronounce
your body burns mine like blue fire
when you try to touch my skin
all your plans collide with mine
destroying any self-love i still hold
your tongue is like daggers coiling
around my neck and killing hope
you brutally pushed me off the cliff
but i survived your evil intentions

–you have no more power over me

after this huge deep love
don't ask me not to write
about what you made me feel
i cannot continue hiding
the words inside of me
because i can only survive
writing this chaotic poetry
transforming my experiences
expressing my emotions
all the passion i still feel
in every cell of my body
but i pretend not to carry
anymore under my eyes

how to survive yourself

i looked you in the eye on that rainy afternoon
while you were caressing my legs slowly
i saw it clearly like the seashore on a calm day
i was gonna lose you soon and irremediably

if we're gonna love each other
in this crazy and terrible way
i only ask that not just memories
remain alive after all this love
if we're gonna love each other
in this irrational and stellar way
i'll try that at least my poems
remain as a witness of this passion

—more than ashes after the end of love

sprinkle

you're the last love of my life

—but just until i fall in love again

how to survive yourself

i just walked into a random bar
and all of a sudden i found love
at the most unexpected moment
you crashed into me like a wrecking ball
and i didn't know how to close the door
to the most powerful feeling in the world

love

this man who i shared a ride with months ago
taught me that everything is possible if you fight
if you create a plan and you follow your dreams
this man showed me that i wasn't crazy or wrong
there are a lot of people like me around the world
bu just t i haven't had the chance to meet them yet
i didn't know in that moment all that those people
were going to impact my life like a hurricane and
change my perspective forever in an amazing way

—be brave enough to live your own life

i'm okay with the fact that
i didn't feel understood there
because that pushed me to jump
of that (non) comfort area and
forced me to learn how to fly

that lead me to where i am
to people i absolutely love
to a changing life in which
i'm truly happy and full
and to this place where
i finally forgave myself

but i cannot forget either
that it changed me into
who i am today
this person
who is damaged
and sometimes sad
and lost
and confused

but is always resilient
and strong
and stunning
and loved

i don't know how it happened
i was just looking somewhere else
distracted thinking about the fact
that i was not being brave enough
to do what it was necessary to
achieve all my biggest dreams

and just like that
you were there
in front of me

and just like that
i was there
loving you

—i didn't even see you coming

we had the most amazing date
in the history of (non) love
we both felt the same way
we saw a sunset by the ocean
we laughed until it hurt
we talked about a life we knew
we would never have together
we dreamed and let the feelings fly
we loved each other in the strange way
you want someone new and ephemeral
and everything felt simple and right
he left that hotel room and i knew
that i would never see him again
that i would never feel him again

but then
on the other side of the world
and just a few months later
i walked down a crowded street
and my eyes suddenly met his

please believe me when i say
sometimes life is awesome

i'm 25 and
to be honest
i have no idea
what to do next
people ask constantly
i give a fake smile
and answer whatever
but the whole truth is
i'm trying to understand
what exactly fits for me
because i have no idea yet;
it's even worse when
anxiety comes and says *hello*
sometimes stress decides to
sleep under my pillow
some nights i cannot breathe
i'm worried about expectations
i don't know how to figure out
what the next step is gonna be
i don't know how
i don't know where
i know nothing
often i feel lost
but i have the key
that can save me:
i know where my home is
simply because my home is me

how to survive yourself

it's been a really long time since
last time i fell in love with someone
i can barely remember how it feels
to be touched by a person who loves you
to sleep next to a body you know perfectly
to feel mutual understanding with just a look
to recognize a smell, a noise, a way of walking

but i hear your voice in the middle of a crowd
and i catch your bright gaze fixed on mine
you get closer and you start talking to me
i smell you and hundreds of feelings wake up

i'm absolutely sure at this point:
my mind is desperately interested in you
even before my body has time to react

–is this love or just attraction?

courage is deciding to move far away
from what you love with your whole heart
just because you want to risk and try that
your most unachievable dream comes true
being brave is knowing you probably
won't be able to get it and even so
keep fighting when it seems impossible

how to survive yourself

what do you do when you find pure love
but you still need to fix yourself first?
i have the constant and painful feeling
that i cannot truly love anyone else
until i discover how can i love myself
in the most sincere and transparent way
what do i do when he's trying to help me
and i keep thinking about how far i am
from what he believes about me?

i adore him
but i still have to find myself first

i was dead inside
destroying me on the outside
i didn't understand what
it means to be alive until
i didn't want to be here anymore
one day i just gave up on life
and then something happened
i'm not sure what made me change
but something hit me with the power
of an ocean crashing against a cliff
and i was able to open my eyes
and see everything that's worthy

i understood why i'm here
why i still want to be here
living and not just surviving:
because i still have things to feel

i'm bent
and broken
and shattered
and wrecked
but all that just means i'm still alive

your eyes collide with mine
and i can see everything
exploding around us
the smile not only
in your mouth
but in your pupils too
butterflies in my throat
fighting to escape
and fly up to you
i give you a grin back
and i'm beyond sure:
i'm gonna fall in love with you

don't be mistaken
i'm absolutely aware of
how lucky i am right now
i live surrounded by people
who remind me daily how
incredibly amazing i am
when i fall and i forget
how to stand up again

friends

yesterday i lost all the conversations and pictures i had on my phone. years and years of memories, lovers, friends, beautiful words, important parts of my reality. and i was feeling, i'll admit it, a little bit sorrowful. but then, a serendipity: i realized that all those memories were not living on a device, but inside of me. all those moments, people, laughs, places, words and feelings are inside of me, floating and vibrating in my cells. for a moment i was scared of myself: *am i more worried about trying to capture life than actually living it?* i don't want to live through a screen that can only hold a minimum part of how i really feel and live and experiment my present. i want to catch those moments and memories and engrave them with fire in my body. so whenever i want to remember i just need to close my eyes and travel there again.

how to survive yourself

stop floating around your past
stop overthinking about the future
and start enjoying this present

time ago i promised
to not fall again
in that hole made of
dreams of future
smiles amidst love
holding hands all night
long kisses on the neck
coffee dates on rainy days
laughing without shame

it was a solid promise
to just love myself

but then you arrived
and i totally forgot why
i was promising that;
you made everything better

how to survive yourself

if you have to make
an important decision
this message is for you:

just follow your intuition
put yourself first
and listen to your soul
the correct answer is inside you

in the exact moment that you don't want something anymore life puts it in front of your face and forces you to look it in the eye.

this is what you wanted. take it
i was eager to have it, but not anymore
i don't care. take it. it's yours now
i learned how to love and expect other things thanks to the absence of what you're giving me now
so you're not waiting for this anymore?
i loved it in the past but today i don't need it
look it in the eye and swear to me you don't want it

what should i do if i have here, within easy reach, everything that i dreamed of in the past? everything that i wanted, loved, needed. now i have the chance to get this goal i fought for during countless nights. but what can i do if i don't feel anymore like that woman who pursued the impossible? what can i do if i learned to love myself just because i didn't find what i was looking for?

no. i don't want it. i don't love it. i don't need it
why?
because now i know exactly how to love myself

how to survive yourself

telekinesis
teleportation
healing
flying
invisibility
super strength
time travel

forget about these superpowers

forgiveness
love
kindness
empathy
respect
compassion
good vibes

those are the real superpowers
everyone should be worried developing

marina aimée

i had to lose myself
in every possible way
to find out who i truly am
it is painful and dark
and scary and lonely
but sometimes you need
to lose who you were
so you can discover
who you are now

they put you in close friends but don't even wave when they see you in the street. they talk about your life but they never bothered to listen to your side of the story. they criticize your clothes and hair because it looks different while they're just copies. they pretend to be nice to you but then they whisper your secrets behind your back. they look at you strange because you're too loud, too happy, too crazy. simply too much. the key is that you're not too much. they're too still, too quiet, too repressed, too sad. they talk, they always will. but the only thing you have to do is to live your life and be yourself. there's nothing better than that.

–freedom

sometimes i'm worried
i'll never fall in love again
i don't feel comfortable
i lose interest quickly
i don't get too involved
but i realized it's not true:
i fall in love every day

with all these pink and purple sunsets
with the fearless laugh of my sister
with the beginning of a new book
with the time i share with my parents
with the emotion when i hug my friends
with good music that makes me dance
with the inevitable enthusiasm of traveling
with the vivid smell and sound of the ocean
with the sun burning my skin on a summer day

i fall in love every day
just not in a romantic way

how to survive yourself

the truth is that we're made out of breathlessness

now that i'm at peace with myself
i understand why i lived in a war
you cannot find serenity
in the things around you
if your mind is in constant
fight against itself
i found calm in my body
and i started to finally live
to love the people who
i'm sharing time with
to feel relieved and blessed
and tremendously lucky
because now i just want to
kiss and love and take care
of this skin that one day
i was trying to kill

deciding that you don't fit in a closet anymore
it's not easy and it's not the same path for everyone
realizing you deserve to be yourself can take time
but when you choose to break the cabinet doors
you start walking and creating your own life
and it feels amazing and relieving and exciting
it's not always going to be easy and you'll find
a lot of people who's not going to understand you
you need to be prepared to lose friends or family
because that can happen, trust me when i say it
but your road is still long and during your life
you'll run across incredible people who will
accept you without you having to hide anything

–coming out

it's perfectly fine to realize
that you're not that person anymore
and you cannot settle again for what
was once enough to fill your soul
change is implicit in everyone's life
you need to evolve and try to be better
you need to leave behind the beliefs that
don't belong to this version of yourself
it's flawlessly balanced to wake up one day
and see that you're completely different
because that only means you're finally
becoming who you honestly are meant to be

i don't care how difficult you think it is
you have to choose yourself this time

i'm full of doubts. i wake up in the morning wondering why i'm here. why am i not fully satisfied? when will it be enough? what if the problem is that i'm not enough? for a moment i just want to run away, to go home and seek refuge in my dad's arms. in my mom's lap. in my sister's smile. but i remain still for two more minutes. i take a deep breath and recompose. i remember why i'm here. because i'm brave enough to not just survive anymore but to take the risk to live with all my heart, with all my possibilities, with all my passion.

–i'm brave enough to miss my shelter and even so stay here

how to survive yourself

if you're struggling with something
this is a message for you:

i know it's hard
i know it seems impossible
i've been stuck and lost and alone too
but trust me when i affirm you can do this
just keep going and fighting and moving
it's gonna be alright

if i close my eyes i can still feel your fingers
drawing fake constellations on my back
i know you could never give me the moon
but you made me feel the whole universe
every time you kissed the tattoo on my ribs
i cannot help but feel grateful to the bone
even if you decided to leave me after that

—because now i know what the universe can look like

i left my city to discover other places
and i came back knowing who i am

everything in this world changes
water flows nonstop
earth rotates every minute
animals evolve and grow
everything is fluid
why are you so determined
to remain the same?
why are you so afraid
of transformation?

he promised to cross the world for me
and i was sincerely in love with him
but not ready for that commitment
i was honestly willing to search him
in another moment
in another place
being a better version of myself
even at the risk that he would
no longer be waiting for me
i can admit it broke my heart
but i learned a lesson long ago:
even if it hurts in the moment
i always need to choose myself

it's not time or distance what
has the real power of healing
it's how you treat yourself
after what happened to you

is all this money honestly making you happy? are you going to buy love with your income? are you going to force people to be kind to you? is it worth it to work from sunrise to sunset not because you need the money but because you want to have more and more and more and impress and buy and believe you're better because of your bank account numbers? are you enjoying your life or just pretending on social media that you're having your best time? is it worth having all that money if you have nothing else?

–you cannot buy with money the best things in life

one man yelled at me and i was quiet
another man hurt me and i only cried
another man lied to me and i believed him
another man broke my heart and i forgave him
another man invaded me and i remained still
another man killed me and i dissociated

but something –everything– changed

one man yelled at me and i screamed louder
another man hurt me and i hit him harder
another man lied to me and i left his home
another man broke my heart and i forgot him
another man invaded me and i raised my voice
another man tried to kill me but i could escape

that's what feminism can do:
literally save your life

blossom

he doesn't deserve
all your tears
your broken heart
your sadness
you deserve better
to experience joy
to feel safe
so wipe your tears
and go dancing tonight
but do it for yourself
not to forget him
do it just because
you need to connect
with your essence again

when i was born my uncles were already there
so i grew up understanding all kinds of affection
because they hold one of the most amazing loves
i've ever seen in my entire life and it's full of
empathy and support and warmth and kind words

i once read a love poem written by a woman
she was talking about another woman's lips
i felt a million things inside my body and mind
but i didn't get what was going on with me yet
because my boyfriend was sleeping next to me

when i was 21 the best person of my life
told me she was bisexual and thanks to her
i could open my eyes to see what i had inside
why i was always feeling disconnected
why nothing was enough for me in my life
she helped me to accept and love my sexuality
now i'm in love with who i am and the way
i understand and live and experiment love

–to all the queer people who helped me understand
who i am and how i want to live

life is not about breathing
and surviving one more day
life is about losing breath
and being genuinely alive

how to survive yourself

i have fulfilled myself with the broken
parts that other people forgot around me
lost and bent parts of who i was in the past
i cuddled all those pieces until they healed
and thanks to the pain others caused me
i could evolve into something stronger
more beautiful and resilient and bright
that is how i created who i am today
that is how i was able to heal myself
that is how i turned something terrible
into the most beautiful thing in my life

after everything i've lived
i learned something that changed
all my contradictory perspectives
all my deepest and unorthodox beliefs
my way to understand my reality

try to live as if tomorrow didn't exist
as if you didn't have another day left
or another chance to say *i love you*
or another opportunity to give that hug
or another shot to take that huge risk

try to live as if tomorrow didn't exist
as if you didn't have another occasion
because you're not sure you'll have it
the only truth you can hold is
here and now

–life is today

how to survive yourself

you'll never find peace
if you don't look inside yourself first

you're the safety net
that avoids all my falls
not the voice of conscience
that asks me to stop
you're the woman
who changed my life
and my true reason
to keep looking
for what i deserve
you're light guiding me
but never blinding me
you shine when you laugh
you become sea when you cry
you push me when i'm scared
because you're sure i'm capable
you blow my dreams
in the right way
so i keep fighting
you're my sister but also
you're my best friend
you're my life partner
you're my treasure
you're my person

i was sitting next to a huge window
with a smoky hot chocolate in my hands
4,5 feet of soft and white snow outside
my body exhausted after hours of skiing
the fireplace lit and warming me up
a poetry book waiting for me on my lap

–a different kind of happiness

i found you in the middle of a personal trip and we had the most amazing days together. we enjoyed an incredible date even though we never planned anything like that. we talked about future and we realized we could have a beautiful life together, even if it was only a dream shared over two glasses of wine. we loved each other in the way you can love someone you just met and you'll never see again. i felt like we were deeply connected. but then you left and i left right after you, absolutely sure that it was the end. however, life had other plans for us and we spent months colliding into each other, finding ourselves again and again. maybe this was meant to be.

how to survive yourself

you deserve someone
who caresses your hair
who tickles you
who cuddles with you
who admires you nonstop
like the masterpiece you are
don't settle for less

i thought i was unable to love
others in the correct way
today i can see perfectly
what my mistake was
i knew nothing about
loving myself fiercely first
so i was expecting others
to fix all my bent parts
instead of feeding my self-love
i was dying for other people

first i needed to love myself without any doubt
first i needed to learn *how to survive myself*

do for yourself all the things
you always do for others

–that's how you blossom

marina aimée

i was inside a box full of insecurities
fear, pain, monsters, lies, screams,
obscurity, blood, hate and tears

one day i was strong enough
to open my eyes and see everything
that was waiting for me outside

one day i was brave enough
to realize that the box was not my life
because my life was waiting outdoors

full of new chances, forgiveness,
love, admiration, peace, blossom
and a big and encouraging sun

life was inside myself
not inside the box

i tried so hard to find someone that could fix all my broken pieces that i misunderstood everything. i spent too much time with people i didn't love just because i was looking inside of them a solution to my problems. ages ago i couldn't be sincerely and fully happy because i was focusing all my efforts, time and energy in the wrong way. but then i found myself. i made amends with myself. i began to forgive myself. and i could see it clearly: i was the solution. the magical love i was desperately looking for had always been inside me. i discovered that between the ruined parts i was also a very bright light. and i understood i had been waiting for years for something that i already had inside. but i'm beyond proud today. because now i can shout to the wind how vibrant, strong and magical i am.

–the true love of my life

if something is about to end
you always try to enjoy it more
seize the time with full hands
live every second and feel it harder
so i wondered for many nights:
why don't we do the same with life?
why don't we live every day like that?
all this is going to end at some point
so let's just enjoy it in the meantime

i don't pretend to live as if nothing hurts me or annoys me or makes me sad. i'm not trying to feign everything is easy or comfortable or makes me happy. but i honestly don't want to face myself as if i were the enemy again. i don't want to face life as if this miracle were a battlefield. i was involved in a war a long time ago. my mind was the enemy. my body was the battlefield. i don't live like that anymore. i learned how to make life easier for myself. how to be at peace. how to breathe without feeling that i'm drowning in the middle of the ocean. i'm not pretending everything is perfect. i'm just trying to live the good moments, to collect all these worthy memories, to love myself like my life depended on it. just because, actually, it does.

my mind was the enemy
my body was the battlefield

it doesn't matter what your dreams are
people will tell you that it's impossible
you'll always find someone in your path
repeating that you're not good enough
but you don't have to care or worry
you just need to listen to one person:
the version of yourself that believes in you
the version of yourself that's sure that
you're worthy and absolutely capable

–trust in the part that has the certainty:
you're gonna get where you want to go

instead of closing your eyes to remember
open them to see what you have right now

marina aimée

you lock your eyes on mine
and everything starts
burning inside of me
i can feel the flames
devouring my heart
my lungs
my stomach
you look at me
the fire menacing
to kill my ideas
my thoughts
my intentions
you glance at me
and i swear to you:
i don't want
to be alone anymore

this city of
cold mornings
sunny noons
and foggy nights
this colorful city
with a freezing ocean
and plenty of dreams
this amazing city
that's a witness
of my growth
my change
my new version
this city,
another place
to call home

San Francisco

marina aimée

not being able to give
your 100% every day
doesn't mean you're not
trying with your whole heart

—rest is essential

i didn't believe
in the law of attraction
or manifestation before
but it's actually true:
you attract your same energy
so vibrate as high as possible
i swear you'll attract
your equal vibes
people who live
and think
and love
as you do

i want to live every second
knowing not everything is perfect
but it's worthy and admirable

i want to live every second
smelling all the small moments
and graving them with fire
in my mind and heart and body

i want to live as if i were truly free
as if i were not tired and empty

i want to feel lucky and blessed
because the only thing i still have
is this very moment

–just here and now

how to survive yourself

i know you're too scared to even move
but you need to take that next step
and then you have to keep walking
because your dreams are waiting for you
i know you're afraid of everything
but you have to believe in yourself
and jump off that comfort ladder
it's scary because you're doing it right
nerves in your fingertips mean it's worth it

marina aimée

they burned us in so many bonfires
that we ignited and allied with the fire
and now nothing can stop the flames

–feminism is an inextinguishable fire

i don't deserve someone who wants to die for me. i deserve someone who wants to live with every cell of their body. a person who wants to dance with me until sunrise. who wants to try food all over the world and be infused with different cultures. who wants to laugh without shame and has the ability to make me laugh until my stomach hurts. who wants to travel by my side and discover every corner of this planet. who wants me as their partner but not as their property. who has a life with me but is able to live without me. who understands freedom in the same way i do. who wants to make all my connections vibrate and give me pleasure without asking anything in return. i deserve someone who wants to live with the strength of the whole universe. someone who understands life like i do. someone who doesn't want to own me but wants to love me in a free, wild, pretty and respectful way. i don't deserve less.

you shouldn't be worried
about improving the opinion
others have about you
but focusing on improving
your own perception of yourself
fight for the person you want to be
keep loving and forgiving yourself
the right people will come to you

–the power of your energy

one day i told my therapist i was scared of being a dependent person because i was always involved in relationships.

it's fine if you want it she said
the problem is i'm scared that i don't want it but i need it i remarked
maybe it's true and you need to feel you're being loved right now she added
but i'm afraid of not being able to be happy on my own i confessed
at some point you probably won't need a romantic relationship anymore, maybe you'll want to be single for a long time. and that will be fine too, so don't be scared of your feelings she declared

and here i am years later, not wanting or needing a romantic love, because i can finally give myself everything i need. i found the path to the best part of myself and i'm too busy enjoying it to share my life with someone who's not my family or friends. and i love this feeling of not needing anyone but myself to be happy and full.

it doesn't matter how hard you fought for it
if it's not making you happy and joyful anymore
you can continue looking for what makes you feel
fulfilled and satisfied and rewarded by yourself
don't settle for something that isn't enough
just because you made the effort to arrive there

—you deserve to be completely happy

loving you is the emotion of a plane taking off
holding my breath in front of an orange sunset
screaming just before the fall on a roller coaster
learning how to love myself next to another person
hiding all the sharpened knives behind the sofa
playing with a sunbeam under the sea water
feeling my chest tingling and about to burst
singing my favorite song in a crowded street
wanting to laugh just because i feel blessed
enjoying the wildness of holding your hand
and being absolutely sure you won't let me go

stop running after people
who have low energy
you actually have the power
of the universe inside you
around you
between you
surrounding you
following you
manifest and vibrate
as high as you can
to make it to the top
use your most powerful energy
to attract what you really deserve

his eyes are made with the water
of all the world's oceans
he looks at me on a lazy Sunday
and i feel the waves of his core
colliding into my body
the shudder of my skin touching
cold water on a summer day
the peace i experience underwater
where i can hear myself better
the happiness of being wild
running crazy through my veins
the laughter i cannot hold
bubbling out of my throat
he looks at me and i feel
the power of the ocean inside of me
his blue eyes remind me of home
and i feel safe and brave
and i feel rash and free
i've always been deeply
connected to the sea
so now that i can perfectly see
the ocean in his blue eyes
i'm insanely attracted to him

masturbation is a special way of healing
you can feel the power between your legs
it's awesome when no one else is controlling you
moving fingers, pillows or toys in that exact place
touching with no hurry to give pleasure to yourself
being aware you have the energy of the universe
in the center of your desires, senses and pleasure

—having sex with yourself
is the most amazing form of love

you'll keep letting others hurt you
until you understand you're worthy
until you learn how to love yourself
until you prioritize your own welfare

how do you explain to your parents that you love them with your whole heart? how do you confess that even so you need to leave them because your happiness is not staying by their side? how do you tell them you're scared to death to be mistaken because then you'd just be losing time? how do you confess to them the euphoria when you discover you were never wrong and this is the life you want? how do you express to them you miss their hugs every day but despite it you don't want to go home yet? how do you tell them that they did great with you and thanks to their love you're now this person full of dreams? how do you admit you're absolutely grateful to them and proud of who they are? i guess you can just write it down and include it in your book. even if it's not in their language. even if your sister will have to translate. even if you know it's not enough.

te quiero, mamá
t'estime, papa

how to survive yourself

it was so hard to spread my wings
that now i don't want to close them again

being able to share my healing journey
and not wanting to hide anymore
is the most amazing feeling in the world
thank you for reading this far
thank you for joining me in this experience

Printed in Great Britain
by Amazon